Book 1
CompTIA A+
By Solis Tech

&

Book 2
Quality Assurance
By Solis Tech

Book 1
CompTIA A+
By Solis Tech

All-in-One Certification Exam Guide for Beginners!

CompTIA A+: All-in-One Certification Exam Guide for Beginners!

Table Of Contents

Introduction

I want to thank you and congratulate you for purchasing the book, *"CompTIA A+: All-in-One Certification Exam Guide for Beginners!"*

This book contains proven steps and strategies on how to prepare for the CompTIA A+ exams.

This eBook will explain the basics of the CompTIA A+ certification and tests. It will also give you some pointers regarding the topics that you need to review. By reading this book, you will gain the knowledge and skills required to pass the tests.

Thanks again for purchasing this book, I hope you enjoy it!

Chapter 1: The CompTIA A+ Examination

This eBook is written for people who are knowledgeable about computers. It assumes that you know to how to use a computer and its peripherals (e.g. printers, modems, etc.). This book will serve as your guide in preparing for the CompTIA A+ exam.

The A+ Certification

This is a certification program developed by CompTIA (Computer Technology Industry Association). This program is designed to provide a consistent way of checking the competency of computer technicians. The A+ certificate is given to people who have reached the degree of knowledge and diagnostic skills required to give proper support in the PC industry.

The A+ certification is similar to other programs in the industry (e.g. Microsoft Certified Systems Engineer and Novell's Certified Novel Engineer). The principle behind these certification programs is that if you need to get services for their products, you want to find technicians who have been certified by these programs.

The Benefits of Being A+ Certified

There are many reasons to get your own A+ certification. The information packet distributed by CompTIA gives the following benefits:

- It serves as a proof of your professional achievement.

- It improves your marketability.

- It gives you excellent advancement opportunities.

- It is now considered as a requirement for other kinds of advanced computer training.

- It encourages customers to do business with you

How to Become Certified

The A+ certification is given to anyone who passes the exams. You are not required to work for any company. CompTIA is not a secret group or society. It is, on the other hand, a group of elite computer technicians. If you want to be A+ certified, you have to do these things:

- Pass the exam called A+ Essentials

- Pass one of the three technician examinations:

- o IT Technician Test

- o Depot Technician Test

- o Remote Support Technician Test

You can take the tests at any Pearson VUE or Thompson Prometric testing center. If you will pass both exams, you will receive a mail from CompTIA. That letter will inform you that you passed the tests. Additionally, it contains the certificate, a lapel pin, and a business card.

How to Sign Up for the Exams

To sign up for the tests, you may call Pearson VUE at 1-877-551-7587 or register online at www.vue.com. For Thompson Prometric, call 1-800-777-4276 or visit the website www.2test.com.

These companies will ask for your name, employer, phone number, mailing address, and SSN (Social Security Number). If you don't want to give out your SSN, a provisional number will be given to you. Additionally, they will ask when and where you want to take the exam.

Obviously, the exams aren't free. You have to pay your chosen testing company. That means you have to specify the payment arrangement during the registration process. You can simply provide your credit card information to the customer representative you will talk to. If you're doing it online, you can enter the credit card info on their payment page.

Who Should Use This Book?

If you want to pass the A+ tests, and do it confidently, you should use this book as a guide for your preparations. The A+ Essentials test is created to measure basic skills for an entry-level computer technician. The technician tests are designed to certify that you have the required skills to service microcomputer hardware.

This eBook was created with one purpose in mind: to help you pass the A+ exams. This guide will do that by explaining the things on which you will be tested.

Chapter 2: The Different Parts of a Computer

A PC (i.e. personal computer) is a machine made up of different components that work together to perform tasks (e.g. helping you write a document or add up large numbers). With this definition, notice that computers are described as having various distinct parts that work together harmoniously. Nowadays, almost all computers are modular. That is, they possess parts that can be replaced if the owner wants to improve the performance of his device. Each part has a specific purpose. In this chapter, you'll learn about the parts that make up a common PC, how they work, and what their functions are.

Important Note: Unless stated otherwise, the terms "computer" and "PC" can be used interchangeably throughout this eBook.

The Different Parts of a Motherboard

The motherboard, also called the system or planar board, serves as the "spine" of a PC. This is the brown or green circuit board that you'll find at the bottom of your computer. The system board is the most important part of a PC since it houses and/or connects the other parts of a computer together.

Different Types of Motherboards

There are two main types of motherboards. These are:

Integrated Motherboards – With this type, most of the parts are integrated into the system board's circuitry. Basically, integrated motherboards are created for simplicity. Since majority of the components are already part of the board itself, you won't have to install them individually. However, this simplicity has a major drawback: once a component stops working, you cannot simply replace it; you have to replace the entire motherboard. These boards are cheap to manufacture but expensive to repair.

Note: If one of the parts breaks, you may just disable it and add an expansion card that has similar capabilities.

Nonintegrated Motherboards – Here, the major parts (e.g. disk controllers, video circuitry, etc.) are installed as expansion cards. You will easily identify this kind of system board since every expansion slot is occupied by a major component.

The Different Form Factors of Motherboards

Computer experts also classify motherboards according to their design (also known as *form factor*). Here are the main form factors being used today: NLX, BTX, ATX, and micro ATX. You have to be vigilant when buying a computer case and system board separately. Some cases lack flexibility: they might not accommodate the system board you will select.

Let's discuss each form factor:

1. NLX – This is the abbreviation for "New Low-profile Extended". In general, this form factor is used for cases that are low-profile. With this design, the expansion slots (e.g. PCI, ISA, etc.) are placed on a special card to reduce the vertical space they occupy. Daughter boards, or adapter cards, that are normally plugged vertically into the expansion slots, are placed parallel to the system board. That means their size won't affect that of the computer case.

2. BTX – This form factor was launched by Intel back in 2003. With this design, the head-producing parts are lined up against the power supply's exhaust fan and the air intake vents. Then, the other components are cooled by installing heat sinks on the motherboard. This design offers a quiet setup since it involves efficient airflow paths and fewer exhaust fans.

3. ATX – With ATX motherboards, the processor and memory slots form a 90° angle with the expansion cards. This design places the memory and processor in line with the power supply's exhaust fan. Thus, the processor can remain cool while it runs. In addition, you may add expansion cards (even the full-length ones) to an ATX motherboard since the memory and processor are not parallel to the expansion cards.

4. Micro ATX – This form factor is similar with the previous one, with one major difference: it is designed for smaller computer cases. Micro ATX motherboards benefit from the enhanced cooling designs of their full-sized counterparts. However, since they are smaller, they have lesser motherboard headers, integrated components, expansion slots, and memory modules.

Processors – Their Functions and Characteristics

Now that you are familiar with system boards, you have to learn about their most important part: the central processing unit (CPU). The CPU controls all of the computer's activities using both internal and external buses. Basically, it is a processor chip that contains millions of transistors.

Important Note: Nowadays, the word "chip" describes the whole package that a computer technician may install into a socket. However, this word was originally used to refer to the silicon wafer hidden inside the carrier (i.e. the "chip" you see on your motherboard). The pins that you see on the outer part of the carrier are connected to the silicon wafer's small contacts. These pins allow you to install the carrier into a socket.

You can identify which part inside the PC is the central processing unit: the CPU is a large square that lies flat on the motherboard with a large fan and heat sink.

The Features of Modern Processors

- Hyperthreading – This word refers to HTT (hyper-threading technology). Basically, HTT is a variant of SMT (simultaneous multithreading). This kind of technology uses the scalar architecture of modern CPUs.

  HTT-capable CPUs appear as two different processors to the computer's operating system (OS). Because of this, the OS may assign two processes simultaneously, such as symmetric multi-processing, where multiple processors utilize the same network resources. Actually, the OS should support SMP in order to use HTT. If a process fails because of missing information caused by, for instance, branch prediction problems, the processor's execution resources can be reassigned for a different procedure that can be conducted immediately. Thus, the processor's downtime is dramatically reduced.

- Multicore – A CPU that has a multicore design contains two processors inside the same package. Here, the OS may treat the CPU as if it were two different CPUs. Just like the HTT, the OS should support SMP. Additionally, SMP is not considered as an upgrade if the apps run on the SMP system are not meant for parallel processes. A good example for the multicore technology is the i7 Quad-Core Processor from Intel.

- Microcode – This is the group of instructions (also called instruction set) that compose the different microprograms that the CPU executes as it performs its functions. The MMX (multimedia extensions) is a special example of an individual microprogram that performs a specific instruction set. Basically, microcodes are at a lower level than the codes used in computer programs. On average, each instruction from a computer program requires a large number of microinstructions. Intel and other processor manufacturers incorporate the MMX instruction set into their products.

- Overclocking – This feature allows you to increase the performance of your CPU, on par with processors created to function at overclocked rates. However, unlike processors created to function on that speed, you have to make sure that the overclocked processor doesn't damage itself from the increased level of heat. You might need to install an advanced cooling system (e.g. liquid cooling) to protect the CPU and other computer parts.

- Throttling – Processor throttling, also called clamping, is the process that specifies the CPU time to be spent on a computer program. By specifying how individual programs use the processor, you can "treat" all of the applications fairly. The principle of Application Fairness turns into a major problem for servers, where each program may represent the work of another user. That means fairness to computer programs becomes fairness to the users (i.e. the actual customers). Customers of modern terminal servers take advantage of this feature.

Memory – Its Functions and Characteristics

Nowadays, memory is one of the easy, popular, and inexpensive methods to enhance a computer. While the computer's processor runs, it stores data in the machine's memory. Basically, the more memory a machine has, the faster it can operate.

To determine the memory of a computer, search for thin sets of small circuit boards that are packed together near the CPU. These circuit boards sit vertically on the computer's motherboard.

How to Check for Errors in a Computer's Memory

Parity Checking

This is a basic scheme used to check for errors. It lines up the computer chips in a single column and separates them into equal bit groups. These bits are numbered beginning at zero. All of the number x bits, one from every chip, create a numerical array. If you are using "even parity", for instance, you will count up the number of bits contained in the array. If the total number is even, you will set the parity bit to zero since the bit count is already even. If the total is an odd number, on the other hand, you should set the parity bit to 1 in order to even up the bit count.

This technique is effective in identifying the existence of errors in the arrays of bits. However, it cannot indicate the location of the errors and how to solve them. Keep in mind that this isn't error correction – it is just a simple error check.

ECC

ECC stands for *Error Checking and Correcting*. If the computer's memory supports this method, the system will generate and store check bits. Whenever the machine accesses its memory, an algorithm will be performed on the check bits. If the result turns out to be zero (or a group of zeros), the information contained in the memory is considered valid and the computer functions as normal. ECC can identify single-bit and double-bit errors. However, it can only correct errors that are single-bit in nature.

The Four Main Types of Memory

- DRAM – This is perhaps the most popular type of RAM out there. DRAM stands for *Dynamic Random Access Memory*. Because of their inherent simplicity, these memory chips are cheap and easy to create compared to the other types. This kind of memory is called dynamic since it needs constant update signals in order to keep storing the data written there. If the DRAM chips won't receive stable signals, the information they hold will be deleted.

- SRAM – This stands for *Static Random Access Memory*. Unlike DRAMs, this kind of memory doesn't require a steady stream of signals. In general, SRAM chips are more complex and expensive than DRAMs. You can use SRAM for cache functions.

- ROM – This is the abbreviation for Read-Only Memory. It is called as such because it prevents the user from editing the memory it contains. Once the data is written on the computer's ROM, it cannot be changed anymore. ROM is usually used to hold the machine's BIOS, since this data is rarely modified.

- CMOS – This is a special type of memory chip. It is designed to hold the configuration settings of a computer's BIOS. CMOS is battery-powered: that means the configuration is retained even if the machine is turned off.

Storage Devices – Their Functions and Characteristics

Computers are useless if they can't store anything. Storage devices hold the information being used, as well as the programs and files the computer needs in order to function properly. In general, storage devices are classified according to their capacity, access time, and physical attributes.

HDD Systems

HDD stands for *Hard Disk Drive*. This storage device is also called hard disk or hard drive. Computers use HDDs to allow quick access to data as well as permanent storage. Typically, hard disks are found inside a computer.

An HDD system is composed of:

Controller – This component controls the storage. It knows how the drive functions, emits signals to the different motors inside the disk, and accepts signals from the sensors within the drive. Nowadays, hard disk manufacturers place the drive and controller in one enclosure.

Hard Disk – This acts as the physical warehouse for the data. HDD systems store data on little disks (about 3-5 inches in diameter) grouped together and kept inside an enclosure.

Host Adapter – This is the system's translator: it converts signals from the controller and hard disk to signals the computer can work with. Most modern motherboards have a built-in host adapter, allowing drive cable connection through board headers.

Floppy Drives

Floppy disks are magnetic storage devices that use plastic diskettes enclosed in a tough casing. Several years ago, floppy disks were used to easily transfer information from one computer to another. Nowadays, few people are using floppy disks because of their small capacity. DVD-ROMs and CD-ROMs have replaced floppy disks in storing and transferring digital information.

CD-ROM Drives

Modern computers use CD-ROM drives. These compact disks are virtually similar to those used in music recording. CD-ROMs allow you to store data for a long period of time. In general, these drives are read-only: you cannot erase or delete the data once it is stored on a CD. In addition, computers need to spend a longer time in "reading" CDs compared to internal hard drives. Why are these drives so popular?

Despite their drawbacks, CD-ROMs are used because they can store large files (about 650MB) and are extremely portable.

DVD-ROM Drives

This is the newest storage device to be used for computers. The DVD (i.e. digital video disc) technology is mostly used for entertainment purposes (e.g. home theater systems). DVD-ROMs are basically similar to the DVDs you use at home. Because of this, computers that are equipped with a DVD-ROM drive can play movies stored on a DVD.

However, DVD-ROMs are way much more useful when used for computers. Since they use newer technology, DVD-ROMs are better than CD-ROMs in terms of storage capacity. On average, DVDs can hold 4GB of data. That means DVD-ROMs are your best option if you are storing or distributing large files.

Important Note: CD-ROMs and DVD-ROMs have the same appearance. The single difference is the logo on the front of DVD drives.

Removable Storage Devices

Many years ago, the term "removable storage" meant something extremely different from what it means now. Tape backup is one of the old storage devices that can still be bought today. Modern computer users prefer the solid-state, random-access removable storage devices. In this section, you'll learn about tape backups and the new storage solutions.

Tape Backup

This is an old type of removable storage. A tape backup device can be installed externally or internally and utilize either an analog or digital magnetic tape to store data. In general, this kind of device can hold more information than other storage mediums. However, they are also one of the slowest in terms of data transfer rate. Because of these reasons, tape backup devices are mainly used for archived information.

Flash Memory

Before, random-access memory chips were only used to access and use data. But now, you'll find them in different physical sizes and storage capacities. Flash memory drives are considered as the best solid-state storage device available. The flash memory category includes SD (secure digital) and other memory cards, USB flash drives, and older detachable and non-detachable memory mechanisms. Each of these storage devices has the capability to store huge amounts of information.

Manufacturers of flash memory devices use revolutionary packaging (e.g. keychain attachments) for their products to provide easy transport options for their end-users.

Chapter 3: How to Work With Computer Parts Effectively

While taking the CompTIA A+ exam, you will answer questions regarding the installation, usage, and replacement of computer parts. This chapter will help you to review regarding those topics.

How to Install, Configure and Optimize Computer Parts

Aside from knowing the characteristics and functions of PC components, you also need to know how to use them. In particular, you should be familiar with the installation, configuration, and optimization of such parts.

How to Upgrade a Storage Device

Storage devices are available in different shapes and sizes. Aside from IDE and SCSI, two of the most popular types, there are SATA (Serial ATA) and PATA (Parallel ATA). You can also differentiate between external and internal drives. This section of the book will explain each of these options.

Preparing the Drive

Regardless of the technology being used, you should format storage devices before using them. Although most drives have their own formatting software, each OS has a tool that you can use. When working with Windows computers, you can utilize the format utility through the command line. If you are working with XP, Vista, 7, or newer Windows system, you can also use the graphical utility program called Disk Management.

How to Work with IDE

Before, IDE (integrated drive electronics) drives were the most popular kind of computer hard drives. Although they are often linked to hard drives, IDE is more than just an interface for hard disks. It can also serve as the interface for different storage types such as Zip, DVD, and CD-ROM.

To install IDE drives, you should:

1. Set the slave/master jumper on the IDE drive.

2. Place the drive inside the drive bay.

3. Connect the cable for power-supply.

4. Link the ribbon cable to the motherboard and to the drive.

5. If the drive isn't detected automatically, you should configure it using the BIOS Setup of your computer.

6. Use your PC's operating system to format and partition the IDE drive.

How to Work with SCSI

SCSI is the abbreviation for *Small Computer System Interface*. This kind of device can be either external or internal to the machine. To configure an SCSI device, you should assign an SCSI ID (also called SCSI address) to all of the devices in the SCSI bus. You can configure their numbers using a jumper or DIP switch.

Whenever the computer sends data to the SCSI device, it emits a signal on the cable assigned to that number. The device will respond with a signal that holds the device's number and the information needed.

You should install a terminator (i.e. terminating resistor device) at the two ends of the bus to keep the SCSI devices working. You can activate and/or deactivate terminators using a jumper.

Here are the things you should do when installing an SCSI device:

- For Internal Devices – Connect the cable (i.e. a 50-wire ribbon cable with multiple keyed connectors) to the adapter and to each SCSI device in your computer. Afterward, place the terminators on the adapter and terminate the final device in the chain. You should leave other devices unterminated.

- For External Devices - Follow the steps outlined above, but here, you should use some stub cables between the SCSI devices in the daisy chain (instead of a long cable that has multiple connectors). Terminate the adapter as well as the final device in the daisy chain (that device should have one stub cable linked to it).

- For Hybrid Devices – Many types of adapters have connectors for external and internal SCSI devices. If you have this kind of adapter, attach the ribbon cable to your internal devices and connect the cable to your adapter. Afterward, daisy-chain the external devices from the external port. Terminate the device at the end of every chain. Make sure that the adapter is unterminated.

External Storage Devices

As capacities shoot up and prices fall down, the number of available external storage devices has increased greatly. Aside from the SCSI variant explained above, you will also see devices with USB connections and those that can connect straight to the system. The computer's operating system will recognize USB devices upon connection. You can just install any additional programs you like to use. A computer program called Dantz Retrospect is included in many storage devices to allow you to utilize external devices as automatic backups.

If the external storage device is linked straight to the system, you can just follow the instructions that came with that product. Then, install additional programs on the computers that you will be using. The main benefit of linking straight to the system is that the storage device/s can be accessed by all of the computers.

How to Upgrade Display Devices

Before linking or unlinking a display device (e.g. a computer monitor), make sure that the computer and the device itself are powered off. Afterward, connect a cable from the computer's video card to the display device. Connect the power cord of that device to an electrical outlet. You may use a modern Digital Visual Interface (DVI) cable or the traditional DB-15 (or VGA) cable.

While installing a new monitor, you should have the proper driver. The driver is the software interface between the display device and the computer's OS. If you don't have the right driver, your monitor won't display what you want to see. Nowadays, you can download the newest drivers from the website of monitor manufacturers.

Aside from the power supply, the most dangerous part to repair is the monitor. Computer technicians say that beginners should never attempt to repair monitors. Monitors can hold high-voltage charges even if they have been powered off for several hours. That means you can be electrocuted if you will try to repair a monitor by yourself. If your monitor stopped working, and you don't want to buy a new one, you should take that device to a TV repair shop or a certified computer technician. The technicians and the repair guys know how to fix monitors properly – they understand the dangers and the correct procedures.

How to upgrade Input and Multimedia Devices

The typical upgrade for input devices is the transition to newer mice and keyboards.

Keyboards

Keyboards may wear out if used repeatedly. The usual problem is "key sticking", where keys are no longer responding to the user. To replace a PS/2 101-key keyboard with a new one, just unplug the old keyboard and plug in the new. As you can see, this is a quick and easy process. Nowadays, however, computer users prefer to replace old keyboards with USB ones.

Here is a principle you need to remember: You can use the "unplug-the-old-and-plug-in-the-new" procedure as long as your computer's OS supports the keyboard you want to use.

Mice

Computer mice also wear out because of repeated use. But don't worry: you can replace old mice with new ones. You may easily replace a PS/2 connection mouse with another without spending too much. As an alternative, you may buy an optical mouse (which prevents dust- and ball-related problems) or a wireless one (which needs batteries to send and receive signals). Although new mouse models still use the PS/2 type of connection, most mouse products in the market use the USB connection.

Chapter 4: The Tools Needed for Checking Computer Parts

The CompTIA A+ exam will also test your skills in checking computer parts. This chapter will help you with that topic by discussing the tools and diagnostic procedures needed.

The Tools Needed by a Computer Technician

A great computer technician needs a great collection of tools. If you are working alone, you may not get past the troubleshooting phase. However, you still need to use certain tools in order to succeed in that task. Once you have identified the problem, you will need to get another set of tools in order to fix it.

This book will focus on the "hardware" tools. These are:

- Screwdrivers – When checking a computer technician's toolkit, you will surely find screwdrivers. Almost all of the big computer parts you'll see today are mounted using screws. If you need to remove these parts, you need to have the right type of screwdriver. This kind of tool is divided into three types:

    o Flat-Blade – Many people refer to this as the *common* or *standard* screwdriver. The screw used with this screwdriver is rarely used today (mainly because the screw's head can be destroyed easily).

    o Phillips – This is perhaps the most popular type of screwdrivers being used today. The screws used with a Phillips screwdriver have enough head surface: you can turn them many times without damaging the screws' head. According to recent reports, more than 90% of the screws used in computers belong to the Phillips-head type.

    o Torx – This is the type of screwdriver you use while working on tiny screws found on Apple and Compaq computers. The screws you remove using a Torx screwdriver have the most surface to work against: they offer the best resistance in terms of screw-head damage. Nowadays, Torx-type screws are gaining more popularity because of their clean and technical look.

- Flashlight – This is one of the tools you should always have. You'll realize how important this tool is when you're crawling under a table searching for a dropped computer part.

- Needle-Nose Pliers – You should have this in your toolkit. This kind of pliers is great for holding connectors or tiny screws (particularly if you have large hands). If needle-nose pliers are still too big to do certain tasks, you may use a pair of tweezers.

- Compressed Air – While working on a computer, you will usually remove the machine's case first. Once the cover is removed, it would be great if you will clean the computer's internal components. The clumps of dirt and fibers can block airflow inside the system unit. As a result, the PC's life will be shortened. The ideal way to eliminate the dust is by using compressed air.

  If you are working for a big company, you probably have a core air compressor that supplies compressed air. If this kind of compressor is not available, you may purchase canned compressed air. However, you'll be shelling out large amounts of money – cans of compressed air are expensive.

- Soldering Iron – You can use it to splice broken wires. Nowadays, computer technicians rarely use this tool. Here's the reason: modern computer parts are created with quick-disconnect connectors. You can easily replace them without splicing anything.

- Wire Strippers – Whenever you have to solder something, you need to use a stripper/wire cutter to prepare the wires for connection. Stripping means you will expose a certain part of the wire by removing the insulation.

- Multi-Meters – This tool is named as such because it is basically a set of different types of testing meters, such as ammeter, voltmeter, and ohmmeter. When used by a trained technician, a multi-meter can identify the failure of various types of computer parts.

  A multi-meter has an analog or digital display, a mode selector switch, and two probes. You can use the switch to perform two things: (1) select the function you want to test and (2) choose the range in which the meter will work. If you need to use an old meter to measure a power pack, you should manually set the range selector. Modern multi-meters, particularly the digital ones, can automatically find the correct ranges.

  Important Note: You should never measure voltage by connecting a manual ranging multi-meter to an AC electrical outlet. This will damage the meter itself, the meter mechanisms, or both.

How to Measure Resistance Using a Multi-Meter

Resistance is the property of electricity commonly measured when troubleshooting computer parts. This electrical property is measured in ohms and represented by the Greek letter "omega." If a multi-meter indicates infinite resistance, the electric currents cannot travel from one prove to another. If you are using a multi-meter to check the resistance and you are getting an infinite reading, there's a huge possibility that the wire is broken.

When measuring resistance, you should set the tool to measure ohms. You can do it using either the selector dial or the front button. Then, connect the PC component you want to measure between the tool's probes. The multi-meter will then show the component's resistance value.

How to Measure Voltage Using a Multi-Meter

This process is similar to the one discussed above, but with two main differences:

1. While measuring voltage, make sure that you properly connect each probe to the source of electricity. For DC voltage, the "-" should be connected to the negative side and the "+" to the positive one. This positioning is irrelevant when measuring AC voltage.

2. You should switch the selector to Volts DC (VDC) or Volts AC (VAC), depending on what you need to measure, to instruct the tool about the voltage you are working with. These settings protect the tool from overload. The multi-meter will blow up if you will plug it into a power source while it's still on "measure resistance" mode.

Chapter 5: Operating Systems

The CompTIA A+ examination will test your knowledge regarding operating systems. Since operating systems play an important role in the computer industry, you should be familiar with them. This chapter will guide you in this topic. Here, you'll learn different things about a computer's OS.

What is an Operating System?

Computers are useless if they don't have any piece of software. Well, you can use them as a doorstop or paperweight – but that is not cost-efficient. You need to have an interface before you can use the capabilities of a computer. And, if you don't know yet, software acts as the interface. Although there are different kinds of software, or computer programs, the most important one you'll ever need is the OS.

Operating systems have various functions, most of which are extremely complex. However, two functions are critical:

1. Interfacing with the computer's hardware

2. Providing an environment in which other pieces of software can run.

Here are the three main types of software that you will encounter in the CompTIA exam:

- Operating System – It provides a stable environment for other computer programs. In addition, it allows the user to enter and execute commands. The operating system gives the user an interface so they can enter commands (i.e. input) and get results or feedback (i.e. output). For this, the OS should communicate with the PC's hardware and conduct the tasks below:

    o Device access

    o Output format

    o Memory management

    o File and disk management

    Once the operating system has performed these basic tasks, the user can enter instructions to the computer using an input device (e.g. a mouse or keyboard). Some of the commands are pre-installed in the operating system, whereas others are given using certain applications. The OS serves as the platform on which the PC's hardware, other pieces of software, and the user work together.

CompTIA A+: All-in-One Certification Exam Guide for Beginners!

- Application – This is used to complete a specific task. Basically, an application is a computer program written to support the commands given to the OS. Every application is compiled or configured for the operating system it will be used for. Because of this, the application depends on the OS to perform most of its basic functions.

  When a program accesses the computer's memory and linked devices, it sends a request to the OS. The machine's operating system will perform the requests made by the program being used. This setup helps greatly in decreasing the programming overhead, since most of the executable codes are shared – they are written onto the operating system and can be used by different applications installed on the computer.

- Driver – This is an extremely specific program created to instruct an operating system on how to access and use a piece of hardware (e.g. webcam, flash memory, etc.). Every webcam or flash memory has distinct features and settings – the driver helps the OS in knowing how the new hardware works and the things it can do.

The Terms and Concepts Related to Operating Systems

In this section, let's define some of the most important terms and concepts. Study this section carefully since it will teach you the terms you'll encounter during the CompTIA A+ exam.

Key Terms

- Source – This is the code that explains how computer programs work. An operating system can be open source or closed source.

    o Open Source – The users have the right to change and examine the code.

    o Closed Source – The users are not allowed to edit or check the code.

- Version – This is a specific variant of a computer program, usually expressed by a number, which informs users regarding the "newness" of the software. For instance, MS-DOS is now in its sixth main version. Computer programmers distinguish minor revisions from major ones this way:

    o "Program" 4.0 to "Program" 5.0 is a major revision.

    o "Program" 5.0 to "Program" 5.2 is a minor revision.

23

- Shell – A piece of software that works on top of the operating system. It allows users to execute commands through an array of menus or a different type of graphical interface. A shell makes an operating system simpler and easier to use by modifying the GUI (graphical user interface).

- GUI – The method by which a user communicates with computers. A GUI uses a touchpad, mouse, or a different mechanism (aside from a keyboard) to interact with the machine and issue commands.

- Multithreading – The capability of a computer program to contain several requests in the computer's CPU. Since it allows an application to perform different tasks simultaneously, computers experience a boost in performance and efficiency.

- Network – A group of computers that are connected by a communication link. A network allows computers to share resources and information.

- Preemptive Multitasking – This is a multitasking technique in which the operating system allocates each program a certain amount of CPU time. Afterward, the OS takes back the control and provides another task or program access to the CPU. Basically, if a computer program crashes, the operating system takes the processor from the faulty program and gives it to the next one (which must be working). Even though unstable computer programs still get locked, only the affected application will stop – not the whole machine.

- Cooperative Multitasking – This is a multitasking technique that relies on the applications themselves. Here, each program is responsible for utilizing and giving up access to the CPU. Windows 3.1 used this method to manage multiple programs. If an application stalls while it is using the CPU, the application fails to free the CPU properly, and the whole computer gets locked, the user needs to reboot the machine.

Conclusion

Thank you again for purchasing this book!

I hope this book was able to help you to prepare for the CompTIA A+ tests.

The next step is to reread this book and use other information sources. That way, you can increase your chances of passing the exam.

Finally, if you enjoyed this book, please take the time to share your thoughts and post a review on Amazon. It'd be greatly appreciated!

Thank you and good luck!

Book 2
Quality Assurance

By Solis Tech

Software Quality Assurance Made Easy!

Quality Assurance: Software Quality Assurance Made Easy!

Table Of Contents

Introduction

I want to thank you and congratulate you for purchasing the book, *"Quality Assurance: Software Quality Assurance Made Easy"*.

This book contains proven steps and strategies on how to implement Software Quality Assurance.

Software quality assurance evolved from the quality assurance in industrial production in the 1940s. With the introduction of computers and the development of applications, it has become an important aspect of software development. In this book, you will learn about the various concepts of software quality assurance and its application in your workplace.

Chapter 1 talks about the definitions of software quality assurance and quality control. It is necessary that you understand what it is so that you can fully grasp the other fundamental concepts. Chapter 2 discusses the ways you can implement software quality assurance in an existing environment. In Chapter 3, you will learn how you can ensure that the software produces quality outputs.

Chapter 4 teaches you how to develop and run software testing while Chapter 5 talks about the timing of the software release. In Chapter 6, you will learn about using automated testing tools.

Thanks again for purchasing this book, I hope you enjoy it!

Chapter 1: **Definition Of Software Quality Assurance And Software Testing**

Software quality assurance is part of the process of software development. It includes the improvement and monitoring of the process. It also follows the processes, procedures, and standards. Furthermore, it ensures the resolution of problems discovered. In effect, it focuses on the prevention of problems.

Software testing, on the other hand, includes the operation of the application or system under controlled conditions, which must include all abnormal and normal conditions. The primary goal of software testing is to know what can go wrong when unexpected and expected scenarios occur. Its focus is on the detection of problems.

Companies differ in assigning responsibilities for quality assurance and software testing. There are organizations that combine both responsibilities to a single person or group. However, it is also common to have various teams that combine developers and testers. Project managers lead such teams. The decision to either combine or separate responsibilities depends on the company's business structure and size. Human beings or machines can perform software testing.

Some projects do not require a group of testers. The need for software testing depends on the project's context and size, the development methodology, the risks, the developers' experience and skill, and other factors. For example, a short-term, low-risk, and small project with expert developers, who know how to use test-first development or thorough unit testing, may not require software test engineers.

In addition, a small or new IT company may not have a dedicated software testing staff even its projects have a need for it. It may outsource software testing or use contractors. It may also adjust its approach on project development and management by using either agile test-first development or more experienced programmers. An inexperienced project manager may use his developers to do their own functional testing or skip thorough testing all together. This decision is highly risky and may cause the project to fail.

If the project is a huge one with non-trivial risks, software testing is important. The use of highly specialized software testers enhances the ability of the project to succeed because different people with different perspectives can offer their invaluable contribution because they have stronger and deeper skills.

In general, a software developer focuses on the technical issues to make a functionality work. On the other hand, a software test engineer focuses on what can go wrong with the functionality. It is very rare to come across a highly effective technical person, who can do both programming and testing tasks. As such, IT companies need software test engineers.

There are various reasons why software may have bugs. First, there is no communication or miscommunication as to the application's requirements. Second, the software is very complex so an inexperienced individual may have a difficult time understanding the software application. In addition, the software may be a big one and includes big databases, data communications, security complexities, different remote and local web services, and multi-tier distributed systems.

Third, there are programming errors. Fourth, the requirements of the software change because the end-user requests for them. In some cases, this end-user may not be aware of the effects of such changes, which can result in errors. The staff's enthusiasm is affected. Continuous modification requirements are a reality. Quality assurance and software test engineers must be able to plan and adapt continuous testing to prevent bugs from affecting the software.

Fifth, time pressures can be difficult to manage. Mistakes often occur during crunch times. Sixth, people involved in the project may not be able to manage their own egos. Seventh, the code has poor documentation or design. It is difficult to modify and maintain codes that are poorly written or documented. Bugs can occur if IT companies do not offer incentives for developers to write maintainable, understandable, and clear codes. Most companies offer incentives when they are able to finish the code quickly. Eighth, the use of software development tools can also result to bugs.

How Quality Assurance Evolved

In 1946, the US Occupation Forces established the Quality Movement in Japan. The movement follows the research of W. Edwards Deming and the Statistical Process Control papers. The methods discussed by the research and papers pertained to industrial production. Each process of production has an output with a required specification and a verifiable main product. The Quality Control group measures the output at different production stages. It ensures that the output falls within the acceptable variances.

The Quality Assurance group does not part in the production process. It audits the process to ensure compliance with the established standards and guidelines. It gives its input for the continuous improvement of the process. In a manufacturing setup, it is easy to differentiate between quality assurance and quality control. These methods become the norm in manufacturing. Since they work in industrial production, they spawned the birth of software quality control and software quality assurance.

Quality Attributes Of Software

Hewlett Packard's Robert Grady developed the common definition of the Software Quality Attributes. The FURPS model identified the following characteristics: functionality, usability, reliability, performance, and supportability (FURPS).

The functional attributes pertain to the features of the software. They answer the question about the purpose of the software instead of its use. The reason for the software's existence is different from the concerns about its reliability, look and feel, and security. The usability attributes are characteristics pertaining to user interface issues like consistency, interface aesthetics, and accessibility.

The reliability attributes include recoverability, accuracy, and availability of the system while performance attributes pertain to issues like startup time, recovery time, system response time, and information throughput. Supportability addresses issues like localizability, scalability, installation, configurability, compatibility, maintainability, adaptability, and testability. The FURPS model evolved into FURPS+ to include specification of constraints like physical, interface, implementation, and design constraints.

The Software Quality Control team tests the quality characteristics. The tests for usability and functionality occur during execution of the actual software. On the other hand, adaptability and supportability tests occur through code inspection. It is not the responsibility of the Software Quality Control or Software Quality Assurance to put the quality attributes into the software. The Software Quality Control team tests for the absence or presence of such characteristics while the Software Quality Assurance group ensures that each stakeholder follow the right standards and procedures during software execution.

In theory, the implementation of FURPS+ will overcome the problems caused by the software's intangible nature because the Software Quality Control team can measure each software attribute. For example, the amount of time it takes for programmers to fix a bug is a measure of supportability. To improve it requires the implementation of new coding standards.

The Software Quality Control group can inspect the code to ensure compliance with the coding standard while the Software Quality Assurance team can ensure that the quality control and programmer teams follow the right standards and process. It is the duty of the Software Quality Assurance group to collect and analyze the time spent on fixing the bug so that it can provide an input in terms of its usefulness to the process improvement initiative.

Chapter 2: Introducing Software Quality Assurance Procedures To An Existing Company

The introduction of the software quality assurance procedures rely on the risks involved and the company's size. If the organization is large and the projects are high-risk, the management must consider a more formal quality assurance process. On the other hand, if the risk is lower, the implementation of quality assurance may be a step-at-a-time procedure. The processes of quality assurance maintain balance with productivity.

If the project or the company is small, an ad-hoc process may be more appropriate. The success of the software development relies on the team leaders and developers. More importantly, there must be enough communications between software testers, managers, customers, and developers. Requirement specifications must be complete, testable, and clear. There must be procedures for design and code reviews, as well as retrospectives. Common approaches used are Agile, Kaizen, and Deming-Shewhart Plan-Do-Check-Act methods.

It is important to evaluate documents, code, specifications, plans, and requirements. To do this, it is necessary to prepare issues lists, checklists, inspection meetings, and walkthroughs. This process is what IT people refer to as verification. On the other hand, validation occurs after verification and includes actual testing of the application. A walkthrough is evaluation in an informal meeting. There is no need to prepare for it.

An inspection is more formal than a walkthrough and attended by at most eight people including a reader, a recorder, and a moderator. Usually, an inspection's subject is a test plan or requirements specification so that the attendees will know the software's problems. The attendees must read the document before attending an inspection so they will find the problems prior to the meeting. It is difficult to prepare for an inspection but it is an effective and least costly way to ensure quality.

Testing Requirements That Must Be Considered

The basis of black box testing is the software's functionality and requirements. A software tester need not be knowledgeable of code or internal design. White box testing, on the other hand, requires knowledge of code. It takes into consideration the code statements, paths, branches, and conditions. Unit testing requires testing of particular code modules or functions. Usually, the application developer performs it because it requires detailed knowledge of the code and program design.

API testing is testing of data exchange or messaging among systems parts. An incremental integration testing tests the application when there is a new functionality, which must be independent to work separately before it can be included in the application. The application programmer or software tester performs this type of testing. An integration testing requires the testing of the various parts of the software in order to know if they work together properly. Functional testing, on the other hand, is a kind of black box testing that focuses on the application's functional requirements. The software testers perform it.

System testing is also another type of black box testing. It includes testing of the general requirements specifications and all the various parts of the software. End-to-end testing, on the other hand, is a macro type of system testing. It includes testing the whole software in various situations that replicates real-world use. Smoke testing or sanity testing is an initial testing to know if the new version is performing well so that major testing can commence. Regression testing retests the application after some modifications or fixes.

Acceptance testing is final testing the software based on customer's specifications. Load testing is software testing under heavy loads in order to find out when the response time of the system fails or degrades. Stress testing, on the other hand, is system functional testing with unusually heavy loads, large complex queries of the database, using large numerical values, and heavy repetition of certain inputs or actions. Performance testing is testing using test or quality assurance plans.

The goal of usability testing depends on the customer or end-user. It uses techniques like surveys, user interviews, and user sessions' video recording. Software testers and developers are not the people to implement usability testing. Install/uninstall testing uses processes to test upgrade, full, or partial install/uninstall of the software. Recovery testing determines how the software can recover in catastrophic instances like hardware failures and crashes. Failover testing is another name for recovery testing.

Security testing tests how the application protects against willful damage, unauthorized access, and the likes. It uses sophisticated testing methods. Compatibility testing tests how the application performs in some environments. Exploratory testing, on the other hand, is an informal and creative testing that does not use any formal test cases or plans. Usually, software testers are new to the application. Ad-hoc testing is almost the same as exploratory testing but the software testers understand the application prior to testing.

Context-driven testing focuses on the software's intended use, culture, and environment. For example, medical equipment software has a different testing approach than a computer game. User acceptance testing determines if the application is satisfactory to the customer or end-user. Comparison testing, on the other hand, compares the software with its competitors.

Alpha testing occurs when the software is almost finished. Usually, end users perform this type of testing. Beta testing is testing when the software is finished and ready for final release. Like alpha testing, this kind of testing is for end users. Finally, mutation testing uses test cases and allows for code changes and retesting using the original test cases to discover software bugs.

Common Problems And Solutions In Developing Software

Software development can encounter common problems like poor user stories or requirements, unrealistic schedule, inadequate testing, featuritis, and miscommunication. Problems can arise if there requirements are incomplete, unclear, not testable, or too general. Furthermore, if the software development has a short timetable, problems can also be evident. If the software does not pass through the testing process, the IT organization will only know of problems if the system crashes or the end users complain.

In addition, problems can arise if the users or customers request for more new functionalities even after the development goals are set. Finally, if there is miscommunication between the programmers and customers, problems are inevitable. If it is an agile project, the problems become evident when it strays away from agile principles.

If there are common problem then there are also common solutions like solid requirements, realistic schedules, adequate testing, sticking to original requirements, and communication. Software requirements must be complete, clear, cohesive, detailed, testable, and attainable. All players concerned must agree upon them. In agile environments, there must be close coordination with end users or customers so that any change in requirement is clear. There must be enough time for design, planning, bug fixing, testing, changes, retesting, and documentation. Each person must not feel burnout during the project.

For testing to be adequate, it must start early. Retesting must occur after each change or fix. There must be enough time for bug fixing and testing. If the end user or customer requests for excessive changes when development has begun, it is important that the project manager explain the consequences. If the change is important, a schedule change is inevitable to accommodate it.

The project manager must manage the expectations of the end users or customer. In an agile environment, the project manager can expect significant change in the initial requirements. There must be a schedule for inspections and walkthroughs. The use of communication tools is important to ensure cooperation and teamwork.

Software Quality Assurance And Software Quality Control In The Workplace

If there is no formal implementation of Software Quality Assurance/Software Quality Control, the quality group can mirror that of an engineering services group. It performs the tasks not done by the development team. It reports to the application development manager. Under this scenario, the manager can instruct the quality assurance personnel to install a load-testing tool and declare him as a performance expert. Although the quality assurance person must perform load testing, it is the job of the software designer/programmer. As such, the software quality assurance/software quality control must be separate from the development team.

Software quality assurance requires the establishment of templates used during reviews. Such templates must have sections for both non-functional and functional requirements. For example, the requirements for performance must be in terms of transaction rates and user population. The use of Traceability Matrix can help in the requirements management. The matrix also encourages the analyst to use individual requirements for cross-referencing.

Software quality assurance verifies that the requirements comply with the templates and that they are not ambiguous. It reviews the risks of non-completion of the non-functional attributes, as well as the Traceability Matrix, to ensure usability of all requirements in other specifications. Software quality assurance can write the test cases, which refer to some of the requirements. It can cross-reference the requirements in the Traceability Matrix.

The interface specification is a requirement if the software is component-based. Software quality assurance must subject the document to verification. It must also subject other lower level specifications to quality assurance if such requirements are critical. Even if there are limited resources for software quality assurance, an IT organization can obtain a good return-on-investment if it pays attention to requirements and interfaces.

Chapter 3: Ensuring Software Quality

Software quality is the delivery of bug-free software within budget and on time. Because quality is subjective, it depends on the customer and his overall influence in the project. A customer can be an end user, a customer contract officer, a customer acceptance tester, a customer manager, a software maintenance engineer, and others. Each customer has his own definition of quality.

A code is good if it works, is secure, bug free, maintainable, and readable. Some companies have standards, which their programmers follow. However, each developer has his own idea about what is best. Standards have different metrics and theories. If there are excessive rules and standards, they can limit creativity and productivity. A design can be functional or internal design.

An internal design is good if the overall structure of the software code is clear, easily modifiable, understandable, and maintainable. It is robust with the capability to log status and with sufficient error handling. Furthermore, the software works as expected. A functional design is good if the software functionality comes from the requirements of the end user and customer. Even an inexperienced user can use the software without reading the user manual or seeking online help.

The software life cycle starts with the conception of the application and commences when the software is no longer used. It includes factors like requirements analysis, initial concept, internal design, functional design, test planning, documentation planning, document preparation, coding, maintenance, testing, integration, retesting, updates, and phase out.

A good software test engineer must possess a test to break attitude, which means that he must be able to focus on the detail in order to ensure that the application is of good quality. He must be diplomatic and tactful so that he can maintain a good relationship with the programmers, the customers, and the managements.

It is helpful if he has previous experience on software development so that he understands the whole process deeply. A good software test engineer is able to appreciate the point of view of the programmers. He must have good judgment skills to be able to determine critical or high-risk application areas that require testing.

A good quality assurance engineer also shares the same qualities with a good software test engineer. Furthermore, he must understand the whole process of software development and the organizations' goals and business approach. He must possess understanding of all sides of issues in order to communicate effectively with everyone concerned. He must be diplomatic and patient, especially in the early stages of the quality assurance process. Lastly, he must be able to detect problems during inspections and reviews.

Qualities Of A Good Quality Assurance Or Test Manager

A good manager must be familiar with the process of software development and must be enthusiastic and promote positivity in the team. He must be able to increase productivity by promoting teamwork and cooperation between quality assurance, software, and test engineers. If the processes require improvements, he must be diplomatic in ensuring smooth implementation of such changes.

He must be able to withstand pressure and offer the right feedback about quality issues to the other managers. He must be able to hire and keep the right personnel. He must possess strong communication skills to deal with everyone concerned in the process. Lastly, he must stay focused and be able to hold meetings.

Importance Of Documentation In Quality Assurance

If the team is large, it is more useful to have the proper documentation for efficient communication and management of projects. Documentation of quality assurance practices is necessary for repeatability. Designs, specifications, configurations, business rules, test plans, code changes, bug reports, test cases, and user manuals must have proper documentation. A system of documentation is necessary for easy obtaining and finding of information.

Each project has its own requirements. If it is an agile project, the requirements may change and evolve. Thus, there is no need for detailed documentation. However, it is useful to document user stories. Documentation on the software requirements describes the functionality and properties of the software. It must be clear, reasonably detailed, complete, attainable, cohesive, and testable. It may be difficult to organize and determine the details but there are tools and methods that are available.

It is important to exercise care in documenting the requirements of the project's customer, who may be an outside or in-house personnel, an end user, a customer contract officer, a customer acceptance tester, a customer manager, a sales person, or a software maintenance engineer. If the project did not meet the expectations, any of these customers can slow down the project.

Each organization has its own way of handling requirements. If the project is an agile project, the requirements are in the user stories. On the other hand, for other projects, the requirements are in the document. Some organizations may use functional specification and high-level project plans. In every requirement, documentation is important to help software testers to make test plans and perform testing. Without any significant documentation, it is impossible to determine if the application meets the user expectations.

Even if the requirements are not testable, it is still important to test the software. The test results must be oriented towards providing information about the risk levels and the status of the application. It is significant to have the correct testing approach to ensure success of the project. In an agile project, various approaches can use methods that require close cooperation and interaction among stakeholders.

Chapter 4: How To Develop And Run Software Testing

To develop the steps for software testing, it is necessary to consider the following.

First, it is important to get the requirements, user stories, internal design, functional design, and any other information that can help with the testing process.

Second, testing must have budget and schedule.

Third, it must have personnel with clear responsibilities.

Fourth, there must be project context to determine testing approaches, scope, and methods.

Fifth, identification of limitations and scope of tests is necessary in order to set priorities.

Sixth, testing must include methods and approaches applicable.

Seventh, it must have the requirements to determine the test environment.

Eighth, it must have requirements for testing tools.

Ninth, it is important to determine the data requirements for testing input.

Tenth, identification of labor requirements and tasks are important.

Eleventh, it must determine milestones, timelines, and schedule estimates.

Twelfth, testing must include error classes, boundary value analysis, and input equivalence classes, when needed.

Thirteenth, it must have a test plan and documents for approvals and reviews.

Fourteenth, testing must determine test scenarios and cases.

Fifteenth, it must include reviews, approvals of test cases, inspections, approaches, and scenarios.

Sixteenth, there must be testing tools and test environment, user manuals, configuration guides, reference documents, installation guides, test tracking processes, archiving and logging processes, and test input data.

Seventeenth, it must include software releases,

The Test Plan

A test plan is a document, which includes scope, objectives, and focus of the software testing activity. To prepare it, it is important to consider the efforts needed to validate the software's acceptability. The test plan must help even those people who are not part of the test group. Testing must be thorough but not very detailed.

The test plan can include the following: the title, the software version number, the plan's revision history, table of contents, the intended audience, the goal of testing, the overview of the software, relevant documents, legal or standards requirements, identifier and naming standards, and requirements for traceability. The test plan must also include overall project organization, test organization, dependencies and assumptions, risk analysis of the project, focus and priorities of testing, limitations and scope, test outline, data input outline, test environment, analysis of test environment validity, configuration and setup of test environment, and processes for software migration among other things.

A test case includes the input, event, or action plus its expected result in order to know if software's functionality is working as planned. It contains test case identifier, objective, test case name, test setup, requirements for input data, steps, and expected results. The details may differ, depending on the project context and organization. Some organizations handle test cases differently. Most of them use less-detailed test scenarios for simplicity and adaptability of test documentation. It is important to develop test cases because it is possible to detect problems and errors in the software through them.

When A Bug Is Discovered

If the software has a bug, the programmers must fix it. The software must undergo retesting after the resolution of the error. Regression testing must be able to check that the solutions performed were not able to create more problems within the application. A system for problem tracking must be set up so it becomes easier to perform the retesting. There are various software tools available to help the quality assurance team.

In tracking the problems, it is good to consider the following: complete information about the bug, bug identifier, present bug status, software version number, how the bug was discovered, specifics about environment and hardware, test case information, bug description, cause of the bug, fix description, retesting results, etc. There must be a reporting process so that the appropriate personnel will know about the errors and fixes.

A configuration management includes the various processes used to coordinate, control, and track requirements, code, problems, documentation, designs, change requests, tools, changes made, and person who made the changes. If the software has many bugs, the software tester must report them and focus on critical bugs. Because this problem can affect the schedule, the software tester must inform the managers and send documentation in order to substantiate the problem.

The decision to stop testing is difficult to do, especially for complex applications. In some cases, complete testing is not possible. Usually, the decision to stop testing considers the deadlines, the degree of test cases completion, the depletion of the test budget, the specified coverage of code, the reduction of the bug rate, and the ending of alpha or beta testing periods. If there is not enough time to perform thorough testing, it is important to focus the testing on important matters based on risk analysis. If the project is small, the testing can depend on risk analysis again.

In some cases, there are organizations that are not serious about quality assurance. For them, it is important to solve problems rather than prevent problems. Problems regarding software quality may not be evident. Furthermore, some organizations reward people who fix problems instead of incentivizing prevention of problems. Risk management includes actions that prevent things from happening. It is a shared responsibility among stakeholders. However, there must be a point person who is primarily responsible for it. In most cases, the responsibility falls on the quality assurance personnel.

Chapter 5: Deciding When To Release The Software To Users

In most projects, the decision to release the software depends on the timing of the end testing. However, for most applications, it is difficult to specify the release criteria without using subjectivity and assumptions. If the basis of the release criteria is the result of a specific test, there is an assumption that this test has addressed all the necessary software risks.

For many projects, this is impossible to do without incurring huge expenses. Therefore, the decision is actually a leap of faith. Furthermore, most projects try to balance cost, timeliness, and quality. As such, testing cannot address the balance of such factors when there is a need to decide on the release date.

Usually, the quality assurance or test manager decides when to release the software. However, this decision involves various assumptions. First, the test manager understands the considerations, which are significant in determining the quality of the software to justify release. Second, the quality of the software may not balance with cost and timeliness. In most organization, there is not enough definition for sufficient quality. Thus, it becomes very subjective and may vary from day to day or project to project.

The release criteria must consider the sales goals, deadlines, market considerations, legal requirements, quality norms of the business segment, programming and technical considerations, expectations of end users, internal budget, impact on the other projects, and a host of other factors. Usually, the project manager must know all these factors.

Because of the various considerations, it may not be possible for the quality assurance manager or test manager to decide the release of the software. However, he may be responsible in providing inputs to the project manager, who makes the release decision. If the project or the organization is small, the decision to release the software rests on the project manager or the product manager. For larger organizations or projects, there must be a committee to decide when to release the software.

If the software requirements change continuously, it is important for all stakeholders to cooperate from the beginning so that they all understand how the change in requirements may affect the project. They may decide on alternate strategies and test plans in advance. It is also beneficial to the project if the initial design of the software can accommodate changes later on. A well-documented code makes it easier for programmers to make the necessary changes.

It is also good to use rapid prototyping if possible so that customers will not make more requests for changes because they are sure of their requirements from the very beginning. The initial schedule of the project must allow extra lead-time for these changes. If possible, all changes must be in the "Phase 2" of the software version. It is important that only easily implemented requirements must be in the project.

The difficult ones must be in the future versions. The management and the customers must know about costs, inherent risks, and scheduling impacts of big changes in the requirements. If they know about the challenges, they can decide whether to continue with the changes or not.

There must be balance between expected efforts with the effort to set up automated testing for the changes. The design of the automated test scripts must be flexible. Its focus must be on aspects of application, which will remain unchanged. The reduction of the appropriate effort for the risk analysis of the changes can be through regression testing.

The design of the test cases must be flexible. The focus must be on ad-hoc testing and not on detailed test cases and test plans. If there is a continuous request for changes in the requirements, it is unreasonable to expect that requirements will remain stable and pre-determined. Thus, it may be appropriate to use approaches for agile development.

It is difficult to determine if software has significant hidden or unexpected functionality. It also indicates that the software development process has deeper problems. The functionality must be removed if does not serve any purpose to the software because it may have unknown dependencies or impacts. If not removed, there must be a consideration for the determination of regression testing needs and risks. The management must know if there are significant risks caused by the unexpected functionality.

The implementation of quality assurance processes is slow over time because the stakeholders must have a consensus. There must be an alignment of processes and organizational goals. As the organization matures, there will be an improvement on productivity. Problem prevention will be the focus. There will be a reduction of burnout and panics. There will be less wasted effort and more improved focus.

The processes must be efficient and simple to prevent any "Process Police" mentality. Furthermore, quality assurance processes promote automated reporting and tracking thereby minimizing paperwork. However, in the short run, implementation may be slow. There will be more days for inspections, reviews, and planning but less time for handling angry end users and late night fixing of errors.

If the growth of the IT organization is very rapid, fixed quality assurance processes may be impossible. Thus, it is important to hire experienced people. The management must prioritize issues about quality and maintain a good relationship with the customers. Every employee must know what quality means to the end user.

Chapter 6: **Using Automated Testing Tools**

If the project is small, learning and implementing the automated testing tools may not be worth it. However, these automated testing tools are important for large projects. These tools use a standard coding language like Java, ruby, python, or other proprietary scripting language. In some cases, it is necessary to record the first tests for the generation of the test scripts. Automated testing is challenging if there are continuous changes to the software because a change in test code is necessary every time there is a new requirement. In addition, the analysis and interpretation of results can be difficult.

Data driven or keyword driven testing is common in functional testing. The maintenance of actions and data is easy through a spreadsheet. The test drivers read the information for them to perform the required tests. This strategy provides more control, documentation, development, and maintenance of test cases. Automated tools can include code analyzers, coverage analyzers, memory analyzers, load/performance test tools, web test tools, and other tools.

A test engineer, who does manual testing, determines if the application performs as expected. He must be able to judge the expected outcome. However, in an automated test, the computer judges the test outcome. A mechanism must be present for the computer to compare automatically between the actual and expected outcomes for every test scenario. If the test engineer is new to automated testing, it is important that he undergo training first.

Proper planning and analysis are important in selecting and using an automated tool for testing. The right tool must be able to test more thoroughly than manual methods. It must test faster and allow continuous integration. It must also reduce the tedious manual testing. The automation of testing is costly. However, it may be able to provide savings in the long term.

Choosing The Appropriate Test Environment

There is always a tradeoff between cost and test environment. The ultimate scenario is to have a collection of test environments, which mirror exactly all possible usage, data, network, software, and hardware characteristics that the software can use. For most software, it is impossible to predict all environment variations. Furthermore, for complex and large systems, it is extremely expensive to duplicate a live environment.

The reality is that decisions on the software environment characteristics are important. Furthermore, the choice of test environments takes into consideration logistical, budget, and time constraints. People with the most technical experience and knowledge, as well as with the deep understanding of constraints and risks, make these decisions. If the project is low risk or small, it is common to take the informal approach. However, for high risk or large projects, it is important to take a more formalize procedure with many personnel.

It is also possible to coordinate internal testing with efforts for beta testing. In addition, it is possible to create built-in automated tests upon software installation by users. The tests are able to report information through the internet about problems and application environment encountered. Lastly, it is possible to use virtual environments.

The Best Approach To Test Estimation

It is not easy to find the best approach because it depends on the IT organization, the project, as well as the experience of the people involved. If there are two projects with the same size and complexity, the right test effort for life-critical medical software may be very large compared to a project involving an inexpensive computer game. The choice of a test estimation approach based on complexity and size may be applicable to a project but not to the other one.

The implicit risk context approach caters to a quality assurance manager or project manager, who uses risk context with past personal experiences to allocate resources for testing. The risk context assumes that each project is similar to the others. It is an experience-based intuitive guess.

The metrics-based approach, on the other hand, uses past experiences on different projects. If there is already data from a number of projects, the information is beneficial in future test planning. For each new project, the basis of adjustment of required test time is the available metrics. In essence, this is not easy to do because it is judgment based on historical experience.

The test-work breakdown approach decomposes the testing tasks into smaller tasks to estimate testing with a reasonable accuracy. It assumes that the breakdown of testing tasks is predictable and accurate and that it is feasible to estimate the testing effort. If the project is large, this is not feasible because there is a need to extend testing time if there are many bugs. In addition to, there is a need to extend development time.

The iterative approach is for large test projects. An initial rough estimate is necessary prior to testing. Once testing begins and after finishing a small percentage of testing work, there is a need to update the testing estimate because testers have already obtained additional knowledge of the issues, risks, and software quality. There is also a need to update test schedules and plans. After finishing a larger percentage of testing work, the testing estimate requires another update. The cycle continues until testing ends.

The percentage-of-development approach requires a quick way of testing estimation. If the project has 1,000 hours of estimated programming effort, the

IT firm usually assigns a 40% ratio for testing. Therefore, it will allot 400 hours for testing. The usefulness of this approach depends on risk, software type, personnel, and complexity level.

In an agile software development approach, the test estimate is unnecessary if the project uses pure test-driven development although it is common to mix some automated unit tests with either automated or manual functional testing. By the nature of agile-based projects, they are not dependent on testing efforts but on the construction of the software.

Conclusion

Thank you again for purchasing this book!

I hope this book was able to help you to understand the concepts of Software Quality Assurance.

The next step is to apply what you learned from this book to your work.

Finally, if you enjoyed this book, please take the time to share your thoughts and post a review on Amazon. It'd be greatly appreciated!

Thank you and good luck!

www.ingramcontent.com/pod-product-compliance
Lightning Source LLC
Chambersburg PA
CBHW061046050326